First Impressions

FIRST IMPRESSIONS

HARRY N. ABRAMS, INC., PUBLISHERS, NEW YORK

HOWARD GREENFELD

Marc Chagall

Contents

1
Life in the Village

Self-Portrait. 1914

This is one of the many portraits of himself that Chagall painted following his return to Russia in 1914.

At the time of his birth on July 7, 1887, no one would have predicted that the first son of Zahar and Feiga-Ita Chagall would grow up to be a painter. Neither of his parents, nor any of his relatives, had ever shown any interest in art. There were no paintings or drawings or prints on the walls of the Chagall home—only a few family photos. As devout Jews, they paid strict attention to the Second Commandment—"Thou shalt not make unto thee any graven images"—which they believed forbade the making of pictures. Because of this, there were very few Jewish painters, and those few lived and worked in the big cities, far from where the Chagalls lived. Nonetheless, Marc Chagall became not only a painter, but one of the best-known and best-loved artists of the twentieth century.

He was born in a wooden cottage in the little Russian village of Pestkowatik, on the outskirts of Vitebsk, near the city of Minsk, not far from the Russian-Polish border. The place of his birth, he wrote humorously in his autobiography, *My Life,* reminded him of "a potato tossed into a barrel of herring and soaked in pickling brine."

When Marc was ten years old the Chagall family moved into Vitebsk itself. It was there that the young boy felt his life really began. Vitebsk, a lively river port and railway junction, with booming small industry, had a population of almost 70,000, half of whom were Jews. It was an old town, and Marc loved to walk down its muddy, unpaved narrow streets, past its many synagogues and churches, its imposing fifteenth-century cathedral, and the rows of gray wooden buildings, many with small balconies, which housed factories and workshops of all kinds. He enjoyed gazing upward, too, at the town's skyline, the pear-shaped domes of its church towers, its corrugated rooftops and steeples and chimneys.

The Chagall home was a modest one. Marc's father, Zahar, a tall, thin, bearded man, had never been and would never become a rich man. Immediately after finishing *cheder,* the Jewish elementary school, he had been apprenticed to a herring dealer, in whose warehouse he worked for the rest of his life, not as a clerk—as his father had hoped—but as a laborer. He knew few pleasures. A pious man, Zahar would get up at six each morning to go to the synagogue to say his prayers. On his return home, he would prepare the samovar and drink his tea, after which he would leave for his job in the warehouse. His long day was spent lifting and moving barrels of salted herring, showing them to customers, and delivering them to the railroad station. He came home each evening exhausted, his clothes shining with (and often smelling from) brine. A shy, quiet man, he had few words for his many children ("I never heard him speak more than twenty consecutive words," Marc later wrote), but he often presented them with small cakes and candied pears, which he took from his pockets.

It was Marc's mother, Feiga-Ita, who sustained the family. A sturdy, energetic woman, who was forced to set up and manage a small grocery store in order to supplement her husband's meager income, she also found time to be an unfailingly warm and loving mother to her children. Marc remembered her as a queen.

There were eight children in the Chagall household, six girls and two boys, but Marc—the first-born—was Feiga-Ita's favorite, just as he was everyone's favorite, a fact no one bothered to hide. Without a doubt there was something special about the dreamy-eyed child with the curly hair.

Chagall's family appear in his early drawings. Though not very proficient, the drawings reveal much about the character of the subjects. Here, the artist's father sits shyly, as Chagall must have observed him countless times. At right is a later drawing that shows Chagall's swift line. Drawn from memory, it perhaps represents his fiddle-playing uncle.

His family adored him. That family was a large one, and it played an important part in Marc's early years. He had his favorites and he wrote of them with humor and poetry in *My Life*. Among them were his tiny, wrinkle-faced grandmother, who always wore a scarf around her head; one grandfather, a butcher who lived in the country village of Lyozno, near Vitebsk, and who was once found on a rooftop eating carrots; and Uncle Neuch, who read the Bible aloud every Saturday and played the violin—like the cobbler he was. And there were other relatives he would also never forget: Uncle Judah, whom he described as looking like a wooden house with a transparent roof; Aunt Relly, whose nose was like a pickle; Uncle Zussy, a hairdresser; and three aunts, who, every market day, seemed to fly over the stalls with their baskets of berries, pears, and currants. He also never forgot the home in which he was raised, a home without toys but one filled with objects that gave him pleasure: the big wall clock, the samovar, and the lamps that brightened his life.

Young Marc began his education at the *cheder,* where he remained for seven years. Most of his time there was spent studying the Hebrew language, the Talmud (the book of Jewish law and tradition), and the Bible. The Bible and its wonderful stories were of special interest to him,

Praying Jew. 1914

Chagall painted several versions of this image of an elderly
rabbi during morning prayers, wearing the traditional
prayer shawl and other ritual garb.

and before long the characters of the Bible were as real and alive to him as were the members of his family and the peasants, tailors, beggars, and bearded rabbis of Vitebsk.

At the age of thirteen, after finishing the *cheder,* he went to public school. He was, unfortunately, not a good student. A dreamer, distracted by his own thoughts during his classes, he enjoyed only geometry and drawing. He did so badly in the other subjects that he was held back a year. After six years, however, as he approached the end of his formal education, he had to make an important decision: what to do with his life.

He knew what he didn't want. He didn't want to spend his days lugging heavy barrels of herring, as his father did. Nor did he want to become a hairdresser or a butcher or a rabbi like other members of his family. He wanted to be something different, but he didn't know exactly what.

He had taken singing lessons and helped the cantor at the synagogue and people said his voice was so beautiful that he often thought of becoming a singer. He had taken violin lessons from his uncle who told him that he was so talented that he sometimes considered going to the conservatory to become a violinist. He loved to dance with his sisters, and everyone said he was graceful, so maybe he'd become a dancer. He wrote poetry in his spare time, and everyone he showed it to was astonished by its beauty, so maybe. . . .

And then one day at school a friend showed him an ink drawing he had made, a copy of an illustration from a magazine. Marc was impressed. If his friend could do it, so could he, and as soon as classes were over he went to the library to look through magazines for subjects that he might use himself. His first drawing was a copy of a portrait of a famous Russian composer. Others followed; he worked on them at school when possible, and he worked on them at home. Before long, the walls of his room were covered with drawings. Though Marc knew that his drawings were getting better and better, no one at home took them seriously; they were child's play. One day, however, someone did take them seriously, a schoolmate who came to the Chagall home, carefully examined the drawings, and exclaimed, with surprise: "You're a real artist, aren't you?"

Marc Chagall never forgot those words; they marked a turning point in his life. "Artist" was a word he had never dared to use, yet when his friend called him an artist it suddenly became clear to him that it was as an artist that he would best be able to express himself. He would record his memories and dreams and visions through pictures, bringing to life on canvas and on paper the objects and people of his world—the flowers, oil lamps, samovars, the soft-eyed cows and the people of Vitebsk, the fiddlers and rabbis and peasants.

There were, however, two problems. Where would he study in order to perfect his art, and how could he possibly convince his mother to allow him to pursue his career as an artist? The first of these was relatively easy to solve. He remembered a large sign that he often passed during his walks through Vitebsk, a blue metal one with white writing that read: "Artist Pen's School of Painting and Design." He knew nothing about the school, but somehow he felt certain that Artist Pen could teach him the techniques of painting and turn him into a real artist.

Convincing his mother—she, and not his quiet father, would have to give permission—to allow him to study painting was another matter. How could he possibly explain to her just why he felt the need to become an artist, how could he get her to take him to see Artist Pen?

He carefully chose the moment to break the news. It was morning, and his mother was alone in the kitchen, putting bread in the oven, when he spoke to her of his plans. She reacted as he had expected—she was so shocked that she almost dropped the bread pan. Her arguments, too, were just what he had expected. For one, Jewish boys simply didn't become painters. For another, he would never make a living as a painter. And finally, what would their family and friends say? But the boy persisted—he *had* to be an artist—and his mother reluctantly agreed to discuss it with other members of the family. Predictably, most of them were

horrified; one uncle even refused to speak to him. But another uncle, the only one who knew anything about art, gave Marc's mother the courage to give in to the boy's request. "If he has talent," this uncle said, "let him try."

So it was agreed that Marc's mother would go with him to see Yehuda Pen. The final decision would be Pen's: if he felt that the boy had talent, Marc could study there; if not, he would have to find an occupation more acceptable to his family.

Trembling with excitement, Marc set out for Pen's studio with his mother. He carried with him a roll of tattered sketches and enough rubles, given to him by his father, to pay for his first lessons—if Pen agreed to teach him. As the boy climbed the stairs to the school, he became intoxicated with the smell of paints. Once they entered the large room in which the classes were held, he was overwhelmed by the sight that greeted him.

Everywhere, there were piles of sketches and drawings; there were shelves of plaster copies of ancient Greek and Roman sculptures—entire statues and heads, and hands, and legs, which the students would be asked to draw during their classes—and there were ornaments and objects of all descriptions, which would be the subjects of drawing lessons and early efforts at painting. There were easels and benches and palettes and paint tables. The room was literally covered with paintings from floor to ceiling. But the paintings on the walls were different from the paintings Marc thought he wanted to do. He instinctively felt that Pen's method was not his—though he didn't know what his was. Yet he also felt certain that Yehuda Pen could help him find the means and techniques to express himself in his own way—if only he would agree to teach him.

After what seemed like an endless wait, Pen entered the studio. A small man, with a blond goatee, he was not the frightening figure Marc had expected; on the contrary, he was friendly. In spite of this, it was a terrifying experience for the would-be student. Too much—all of Marc's future, it seemed—depended on this one teacher's reaction to his work, and the boy's hands shook as he unrolled the drawings he had worked so hard on.

When he returned to Russia in 1914, Chagall set out to record every detail of life in his hometown. This street scene, drawn in pencil and ink, is one of many.

Pen thumbed through them without expression. Neither the boy nor his mother could guess his reaction until he reached the last sketch and said what Marc hoped he would: "Yes, he has some ability."

It wasn't much—Pen wasn't really enthusiastic and didn't promise them that Marc would some-day be a great artist—but it was enough. Pen had to be taken seriously by Marc's family. They had learned that he was one of the few Jews of Vitebsk to have studied at the great Academy in St. Petersburg (now known as Leningrad), the center of all artistic activity in Russia. Besides, an agreement was an agreement. The boy's family now had to consent to his enrolling in Artist Pen's School of Painting and Design.

The classes at the school marked the young man's entry into the world of art, but aside from that they were disappointing. As he had guessed the first day when he looked at the paintings on the wall of the studio, young Chagall soon realized that he could never paint the way Pen did. Teacher and

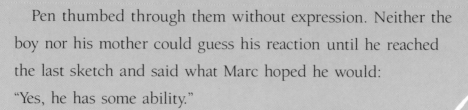

pupil expressed themselves in different ways. Pen approached his subjects the way a photographer would. His paintings were lifelike, accurate, and realistic. Chagall's were different. He was not interested in merely reproducing on canvas or paper an accurate likeness of the subjects of his paintings. Pen's subjects looked on canvas the way they looked to everyone. Chagall's looked the way they looked only to Marc Chagall.

In spite of their sharp differences, Pen was unfailingly kind to his pupil. He understood him well enough to allow him to work alone, in his own way, without supervision. For a while he even let him attend classes without charge. But after a few months, Chagall realized it was useless for him to continue. There was little he could learn from his kindly teacher.

His time at Pen's, however, had not been completely wasted. He had learned the techniques of painting—how to prepare a canvas with a layer of gesso as a ground on which to paint, how to mix colors to obtain the desired tints and shades, how to use a palette knife to apply thick pigment, how to use the various oils and paint thinners to keep his colors liquid, and how to clean his brushes so they would be fresh the next day. But, in addition to these skills, it was also in Pen's classes that Marc was able to meet and befriend other young people from a world he had never known, who shared his interest in and passion for art. Chief among these was Victor Mekler, a sensitive young man who came from one of Vitebsk's wealthier families. Understanding Pen's limitations as a teacher, Victor asked Marc to give him lessons outside of school, believing that his friend could show him

In 1911, after a year away from home, Chagall drew these portraits of his parents from memory, adding a grimacing sketch of himself probably drawn in front of a mirror.

things that he could never learn from the older man. Marc was flattered, and he agreed. However, although he badly needed the money, he refused any payment from Victor who was, above all, a friend.

Their friendship, based largely on a shared enthusiasm for art, flourished. The two spent hours together, painting and talking, at Victor's parents' home in Vitebsk and in their spacious country house outside the city. In time, however, Victor realized that he had learned all he could in Vitebsk. He informed Marc that he had decided to move to the great capital city of St. Petersburg, about three hundred miles to the north, to continue his studies, and he urged his friend to join him on what would be an exciting adventure.

It was, Marc knew, a wonderful idea, a move he felt he would have to make at some point in his life if he really wanted to succeed as a painter. But he was, understandably, afraid. A move would mean having to give up a job he had held for some time as an apprentice to a photographer, where his duties consisted of retouching photographs, correcting mistakes, removing blemishes. The work bored him, but by doing it he was acquiring a skill that would enable him to make money in the future.

Photographers—whose main business in those days was making portraits—could always earn a living while painters rarely could. As a photographer, he would always have a roof over his head and enough food to eat, while as a painter he knew he would have to struggle. Yet none of this mattered; security was of no importance to the determined young man. He wanted to become a painter and not a photographer, no matter how uncertain the future or how great the risks.

Nonetheless, the risks—and the obstacles—he faced in moving to St. Petersburg were enormous. Above all, there was the very real chance of starvation. Unlike Victor, Marc had no rich family to support him while he studied. In fact, all his father could give him was a small sum that would last only for a short time. He would quickly have to find a way to earn money in order to survive.

Equally difficult was the problem of obtaining official permission to remain in St. Petersburg. Under the rule of the Czars—the emperors who governed Russia—Jews were treated harshly. They were considered outsiders and needed special authorization to live in the capital. Although permitted to settle in the provinces, in towns like Vitebsk in the south and west of Russia, they were not allowed to live in its major cities without fulfilling certain requirements. Because of this, the necessary permits were difficult to obtain. Usually they were granted only to members of certain professions, doctors and lawyers, for example, their household workers, and sometimes to other people employed by them. Chagall was none of these. But in special circumstances, a merchant in a provincial town could delegate someone to do business for him in St. Petersburg for a short period of time. Under this ruling, Chagall's father was able to obtain, from a shopkeeper friend, a temporary certificate stating that Marc Chagall had been commissioned to bring goods for him to and from St. Petersburg.

— 2 —

The Training of an Artist

Provided with a temporary permit to enter the city, and carrying the small amount of money his father had given him, Marc Chagall arrived in St. Petersburg determined to make his way as a painter. It was the winter of 1906–07, and he was nineteen years old. The contrast between his hometown of Vitebsk and the great city was enormous. Though a bustling town, Vitebsk was really no more than a provincial capital, and a rather unexciting one. St. Petersburg at the time was the capital of all Russia (Moscow became the capital in 1918), and was one of the world's great cities. It was alive with art,

music, and theater. Not isolated as was Vitebsk, its attitudes and way of life were influenced by the new ideas and currents of change in the arts that were sweeping through Western Europe.

Chagall's stay there—he lived in the capital, on and off, for three years—was ultimately rewarding, but his first months were difficult and often heartbreaking. As expected, his father's gift was used up in a very short time, and he was only able to earn a small amount of money, again working as a photo retoucher. He was often cold and hungry. He depended on the kindness of some wealthy art patrons he had met through Yehuda Pen and through Victor Mekler, one of whom gave him a regular allowance for a few months. But this hardly sufficed.

Furthermore, finding a place to live, and keeping it, was a continuing concern, and he never had a room of his own. He was forced, instead, to share quarters with others. He remembered some of these vividly in his autobiography. Among them were a young sculptor who "roared like a wild animal and hurled himself

furiously on his clay to keep it from drying out," a kind laborer with a deep-black mustache who flattened himself against the wall so that Chagall might have more space in the bed they shared, a roommate whose snoring kept him awake all night, and a drunken typographer who played the accordion in an amusement park at night.

An equally disturbing problem during the first part of his stay in the capital was obtaining legal permission to remain there permanently. The authorization that had been arranged by his father was good for only a few months and could not be renewed. Hard as he tried, every other attempt to obtain a permit failed. Once, upon returning to St. Petersburg from Vitebsk, where he traveled often, he was jailed for trying to enter the capital without a permit. Out of jail, he realized that his only hope was to learn a profession that would qualify him for status as a permanent resident. His search led him to a sign painter who needed an apprentice-assistant, but after months of hard work, Chagall was unable to pass the final examination which would have qualified him to work and thus entitle him to the necessary permit.

With good reason, Chagall was becoming desperate. He knew that he had to remain in St. Petersburg in order to grow as an artist—a return to Vitebsk was unthinkable. Yet he was unable to do so legally, and he could not risk going to jail again—one stay there was enough. Just when all seemed hopeless, however, his luck changed. He met a kindly and wealthy lawyer named Goldberg, who proved to be his guardian angel. Goldberg was not only a patron of the arts who admired Chagall's skills, he was also a man of ingenuity. He offered the young painter a solution to his practical problems. As a professional, the lawyer was permitted to hire Jewish servants and offer them a place to live in his own home, at the same time obtaining permanent residence permits for them. No one, he reasoned, could prevent him from "hiring" Chagall and allowing him to live in the Goldberg residence. He couldn't offer him a real room of his own—only a bed in a small alcove under the stairs—but it was enough.

Chagall finally had a home and was legally permitted to remain in St. Petersburg. Goldberg and his family were of immense importance to the likeable young painter. They introduced him to their friends, and they even bought some of his drawings in order to encourage him. More than that, Goldberg would soon be instrumental in finding Chagall a place in the art school best suited for his needs.

The quest for such a school had been among Chagall's most serious tasks. Following his arrival in St. Petersburg, he had thought of applying to the Imperial Academy of Art. Considered the finest art school in the capital, the Academy would also have solved a problem for Chagall, because admission there automatically entitled the student to a resident's permit. But Chagall knew there was no use in even making an application: he lacked the proper diploma from high school, and, besides, the Academy rarely accepted Jewish applicants—Pen had been an exception.

A possibility that offered greater hope was Baron Stieglitz's School of Applied Arts. Since all students at that school also received permission to remain in the capital, Chagall went there as soon as he arrived in the city. But his application was rejected. The drawings he had to make—of a plaster model of a wine glass with a bunch of grapes—as part of the entrance examination failed to meet the standards of the school's board of experts. His drawings were not sufficiently precise; they showed his personal impression of the subject and not the exact copy expected by the board.

Finally, Chagall applied and was accepted by a school sponsored by the Imperial Academy for the Protection of the Arts, created for students who had failed to gain admission to the Academy. His work there was so promising and original that it attracted the attention of the school's dynamic new director, Nicholas Roerich, a painter, poet and archeologist, who rewarded the young man by granting him a small scholarship. Chagall was overjoyed; he was now "rich" and could afford to have a real meal almost every day in a cheap restaurant.

In spite of this, he was unhappy. Although most of his teachers praised him, he felt that the time spent in the school's damp classrooms was wasted. He worked hard, but he understood better than his teachers could that he was really making no progress. Finally, in July 1908, after having been ridiculed by the one teacher who did not appreciate his work, he abruptly left the school—not even bothering to collect the rest of his scholarship money.

There was one last hope in his search for a congenial place to learn his craft. Through his benefactor Goldberg, Chagall had met many art collectors, several of them active in efforts to promote a rebirth of Jewish culture in Russia. One of them, who had recognized his talent, was Leopold Sev, the editor of an important Jewish cultural magazine. Through Sev, Chagall first heard of Leon Bakst and his classes at the Svantseva School. The Svantseva was a different kind of art school, the most liberal in Russia, and the most open to and influenced by the new ideas of modern art that were sweeping through Western Europe, most of them originating in Paris. Bakst, who had worked and lived in Paris, was also a different kind of teacher and it was clear to Sev that under his guidance at the Svantseva School, young Chagall could flourish as an artist.

Through Sev, Chagall was given an appointment to show his work to Bakst since without the teacher's approval, it would be impossible for him to study at the Svantseva. Armed with a letter of recommendation, he arrived at Bakst's home. Their first meeting, a crucial one, was successful. Bakst, whose origins were as humble as Chagall's—he came from a small town not far from Vitebsk— was a friendly man, whose warm smile immediately put Chagall at ease. And his response to the sketches was encouraging: he agreed to admit him to the school

It didn't take Chagall long to realize that this new school was unlike any he had attended in the past. It was vibrant and alive, far more stimulating than he had believed a school could be. The teachers challenged him as he had never been challenged before, and the other students were on a higher level than those with whom he had studied before. Among these were the daughters of Leo

Tolstoy, the great author of *War and Peace,* and Vaslav Nijinsky, who was to become one of the greatest ballet dancers of all time and whose easel was next to Chagall's.

The program at the school consisted of classes in painting and drawing, both from models and from memory. The students would work all week, and on Fridays Bakst would come to see their paintings and drawings and comment on them. His criticisms, made after carefully examining the work of each pupil as the rest of the class watched and listened closely, were severe. He showed no pity as he pointed out their faults. Chagall's first weeks did not go well. On the first Friday, Bakst studied one of his efforts; the teacher's remarks were harsh and unsympathetic. Understandably, Chagall was upset—no one had ever judged him in such terms. The following Friday, however, was even worse, for Bakst merely passed by his work in silence, as if it was not even worthy of comment.

This was too much. Doubting his ability to learn and take advantage of what Bakst had to offer, Chagall decided to leave school and work on his own— until he felt he was ready to return. It was a difficult period of self-evaluation, during which he painted day and night. After three months, he returned to the school, confident enough to subject himself once again to Bakst's criticism. His confidence was justified. On the first Friday following his return he showed his latest work to the teacher, who

Russian Wedding. 1909

Chagall painted this picture from memory, a wedding procession
seen years before. Beside a strolling fiddler, evidently hired for
the occasion, walks the rabbi; behind him are the bride and
groom followed by friends and relatives. Even with the merry
fiddler the scene looks rather somber for what should be a
festive event.

this time was so pleased that he hung the painting on the wall of the studio.

While studying at the Svantseva School, Chagall's work improved, influenced both by his classes with Bakst and by his first exposure—in printed reproductions—to the paintings of Paul Cézanne, Vincent Van Gogh, Paul Gauguin, and Henri Matisse, artists who were changing the course of art history by their bold, new approaches to painting. Bakst was impressed by his progress. "What I like about him," he wrote later, "is that after listening closely to my lessons he takes his paints and brushes and does something absolutely different from what I have told him." Chagall was gradually developing a style of his own, using increasingly vivid colors instead of muted shades to portray his subject matter, scenes drawn from his hometown and his childhood. Two examples of this are among his earliest masterpieces, the gentle and poetic *Russian Wedding* and the haunting and powerful *The Dead Man.* And he was also, with good reason, beginning to take himself seriously as a painter. His *Self-Portrait with Brushes,* painted in 1909, shows the twenty-two-year-old Chagall as he saw himself then: a painter—undeniably and assertively a painter—with a traditional beret on his head and three brushes in his hand, smiling a mysterious smile of self-confidence and superiority.

Most of Chagall's early paintings are autobiographical, based on memories of his childhood in Vitebsk. While living in St. Petersburg, he gradually outgrew Vitebsk, but it remained forever a part of his universe, and during his three-year stay in the capital he often visited and spent long periods in the town of his youth. One such visit was of special importance, for during it he met Bella Rosenfeld, the first love of his life.

They first met in the autumn of 1909. During his visits home, Chagall spent more and more time with new friends, not those of his early childhood, but those he had met through Victor Mekler: young intellectuals familiar with and enthusiastic about the world of art, music, and literature. Among these was Thea Brachman, the daughter of a wealthy physician. Chagall liked Thea and he spent many hours at the Brachman home. In contrast to his own, it was a house filled with music and flowers, with singing birds, and a friendly dog. It was a place alive with the conversation of young, vital people among whom the painter felt at ease.

It was there that Chagall met Bella, the youngest daughter of one of the richest families of Vitebsk—her father owned three jewelry shops. She was an aspiring actress who was studying at one of the best girl's schools in Moscow. When he saw her, it was love at first sight: "Her pale coloring, her eyes. How big and round and black they are! They are my eyes, my soul. . . . I know this is she, my wife." And when he heard her speak, he wrote in *My Life,* he found her voice to be "like that of a bird from some other world."

For Bella, too, this meeting was unforgettable. Marc Chagall was not the first artist she had met. On trips to Berlin, Vienna, and Marienbad, a popular resort where her family spent many summers, she had met all kinds of people, among them many artists. But there was something special about this Marc Chagall. In her own memoirs, Bella compares him to a twinkling star. He was handsome and he was strong, she remembered, but he seemed to have no feet, seemed in some way to be floating.

Following their first meeting, Marc and Bella saw each other frequently. They shared each other's thoughts and feelings as neither had ever done before. They were both shy, and in the beginning they held their meetings in secret. Before long, however, it didn't matter who knew about them. They were in love. Each

Portrait of My Fiancée in Black Gloves. 1909

Chagall's first painting of Bella, his future wife, shows the work of a romantic twenty-two-year-old, in love for the first time. In his eyes she is strikingly beautiful and her pose reveals her to be a young woman of uncommon strength and intelligence. What can we learn about her from the way she is dressed?

time Marc came to Vitebsk for a visit, it was Bella he sought first. She inspired him and she encouraged him, by gently and sensitively criticizing his work. And he immortalized her in many of his paintings, one of which, *Portrait of My Fiancée in Black Gloves,* remains among his finest.

When Marc proposed that they become formally engaged, Bella accepted joyously. She had no doubts. Her family, however, disagreed. The Rosenfelds and the Chagalls belonged to different classes. The Rosenfelds lived in a beautiful home; they had servants. Their daughter, Bella, was not only beautiful, she was also brilliant. Upon graduation from high school she had been given a gold medal as one of the four outstanding graduates in all of Russia. How, they wondered, could such a brilliant girl from such a brilliant family even consider marrying a young man from a poor family whose only desire was to become a painter?

None of this mattered to the young couple. They knew they belonged together, and they knew they would someday wed. But they also knew — given her family's objections — that they would have to wait until Marc had proven himself and made his way as a painter.

In 1910, Chagall took a giant step in that direction. Certain, because of what he had learned at the Svantseva School, that his art could not grow and flourish in Russia, where true artistic experimentation was discouraged, if not prohibited, he decided to leave St. Petersburg for Paris, the vital center of the world of modern art. "My art needed Paris like a tree needs water," he commented. He had long considered such a move. Then, his teacher, Bakst, announced his own intention to leave for the French capital. He had been summoned to work as a scenic designer for the great impresario Sergei Diaghilev, whose ballet company was showing the world the glories of Russian dancing. Chagall, too, decided to make the move.

It was a difficult decision, requiring both courage and money. Chagall had much of the former and little of the latter. At first, he thought Bakst might help by hiring him as an assistant, but after taking lessons, at Bakst's suggestion, in the art of painting scenery, he was given a test which he failed. On the basis of this failure, Bakst not only refused to hire him, but also advised the young painter to abandon his plans to go to Paris under any circumstances, warning that he would most likely starve in the French capital.

In spite of this warning, Chagall persisted, searching for a sponsor who might make the move to Paris possible. Before long, he found one, Maxim Vinaver, a distinguished lawyer and member of parliament, and Leopold Sev's brother-in-law. Vinaver believed in Chagall and his art and promised him an allowance that would enable him to live in Paris. Chagall never forgot him and his generosity. "My father put me into the world, Vinaver made a painter of me," he wrote in his autobiography. "Without him, I would probably have remained a photographer in Vitebsk without any idea of Paris."

As he prepared to leave Vitebsk and Russia behind him, he was nervous. He even urged his parents to join him, but they refused. He was twenty-three years old, they pointed out, and he would have to be on his own. In the summer of 1910, he left his hometown and his family. And he left Bella, certain that their love would endure and that they would once more be together. He gathered all of his possessions, his paintings and his drawings, and he boarded the train for the four-day journey to Paris.

— 3 —

Reborn in Paris

Paris Through the Window. 1913

Chagall's delight in his adopted city is expressed in this joyful painting. He appears himself with two faces, one facing forward and the other back, reflecting his status as a man with two homes—France and Russia.

When Marc Chagall first arrived in Paris, in August 1910, he felt lost. He was confused by the traffic and the masses of people, all speaking a foreign language he barely understood. And he was dazzled by the brilliant colors and lights, so different from the drab grayness of his hometown. In fact, only the great distance that separated him from Russia prevented him from returning there during his first week. He eagerly sought any excuse to give up his courageous adventure. Before long, however, after he had had a chance to visit the city's magnificent museums and galleries, he no longer felt alone. He came to realize that Paris was his second Vitebsk, his second birthplace.

He felt most at home in the Louvre, the enormous art museum along the River Seine. As he studied the paintings of the great French masters—Eugène Delacroix, Gustave Courbet, Antoine Watteau, Jean-Baptiste Chardin—and others, he felt he was visiting old friends, who gave him the strength and courage to continue his struggle to become an artist. Visits to smaller galleries and museums followed, and there he came to know at first hand the work of the contemporary painters he had learned about at the Svantseva School. The paintings of these men, many of whom were experimenting and creating new forms of art, inspired him to work in his own way and to express his unique personal vision. Though he was to study from time to time at various Parisian art schools, it was from seeing the works of Cézanne, Picasso, Braque, Matisse and, even more, from the city of Paris itself that the young man learned his lessons. "I was very dark when I arrived in Paris," he said years later. "I was the color of a potato . . . Paris is light." And that light, during his first years in the French capital, shone through his work and intensified his colors.

At the time of Chagall's arrival, and from 1910 to 1914—the years he lived there—many thousands of artists from all over the world came to Paris, which more than any other city encouraged artistic activity. They came, usually at great personal sacrifice, to be inspired by the vitality and spirit of Paris. And they were willing to live in dark, dingy cramped quarters on near-starvation diets to do so. Because of the allowance given him by Vinaver, Chagall was far better off than most. Starvation and homelessness were never serious threats, yet his struggle to survive, especially during his first months, was often difficult. Sometimes he lacked money to buy new canvases, but nothing could stop him from working. He would buy old paintings, which cost less than fresh canvas, and paint over them. Sometimes, too, when money was in short supply, he was unable to pay for a full meal, but that presented no real problem; a piece of bread, given him by a sympathetic baker, and a cup of coffee would suffice. Most important, he had Paris, more than sufficient nourishment for the artist. For him, the city meant "light, color, freedom, the sun, the joy of living," he wrote.

He was never without a place to live. His first home, a room rented to him by a Russian painter, was ideally located in the midst of Montparnasse, the lively section of the city that housed most of its artists and writers. At its center were two famous cafés, the Dôme and the Rotonde, meeting places where, around crowded tables, drinking coffee or wine, German and Russian and American and Polish painters would join their French colleagues in stimulating discussions of the latest trends and movements in art. Chagall enjoyed observing these encounters, but he rarely joined in. Much as he loved to paint and much as he appreciated great painting, he rarely liked to talk about his art. He had no theories or rules. Painters have always been mad, he felt, and there was no reason to expect them to talk sense.

In spite of this, he did get to know the important artists and writers of Paris, and he did learn and profit from his meetings with them. He especially enjoyed his visits with Sonia and Robert Delaunay, two artists with whom he formed a lasting friendship. On Friday evenings he regularly went to the home of Riciotti Canudo, the editor of an avant-garde magazine, where he had a chance to meet some of the same painters whose work he was seeing in the city's galleries.

Even more opportunities to become acquainted with artists like himself—

those struggling to find places in the world of art—came in the winter of 1912 when Chagall moved into a twelve-sided building known as La Ruche, or The Beehive. Founded at the turn of the century by a little-known sculptor whose dream had been to establish inexpensive lodgings and studios for impoverished creative artists, La Ruche is today remembered as a cradle of modern art.

Chagall's studio—one of 140 in a complex which included not only The Beehive but also additional buildings the sculptor had bought—was on the top or second floor of the main building. The neighboring studio was occupied by Amedeo Modigliani, a young Italian who would be recognized as one of the most important artists of his time. Among other members of this community of artists were painters and sculptors of equal importance, a number of them Jews from Russia and Poland.

For most of these artists, La Ruche was a center of social activity as well as a place to work. They sang together, recited poetry, and played guitars throughout the night, often loudly. They discussed art, politics, life itself and its meaning, until sunrise. But Chagall was a loner. While the others enjoyed themselves, he remained in his room, working feverishly by the light of a small kerosene lamp. In his autobiography, he describes his room as a picture of total confusion. On the floor lay paintings, drawings, eggshells, and empty soup cans. On the shelves, reproductions of the works of Paul

Self-Portrait with Seven Fingers. 1912

According to a Yiddish saying, doing something with
seven fingers means doing it well. Here, a confident
Chagall paints a scene of his hometown, Vitebsk, while
out the window Paris beckons.

I and the Village. 1911

In this painting are many puzzling images; why is the man's face green and why is he wearing a cross? The artist did not explain his paintings, so the questions remain.

Cézanne and El Greco were propped up next to the remains of herring and stale crusts of bread. None of this mattered; the young man from Vitebsk had only one passion — his art. Neatness, parties, and intellectual discussions only distracted him from this, his reason for living. Nothing and no one could stop him from painting — neither the sounds from his neighbors' rooms nor the cries from a nearby slaughterhouse, which must have reminded him of the sounds he had heard at his grandfather's butcher shop back in Russia.

Chagall's friends and neighbors, at La Ruche and elsewhere, considered him a strange "poet," whose paintings — their themes and his treatment of them — set him apart from his fellow artists. He was developing a style that was to remain his own, that would enable us to know that a Chagall painting was a Chagall painting and could have been created by no one else. His works, often expressing memories of Russia, its folk heritage and his own childhood, were seldom completely realistic. Instead, they were dreamlike: lovers or cows or donkeys or fish defying gravity and logic by floating miraculously in the air.

Everyone began to notice, too, his extravagant, imaginative use of color. Even his former teacher Léon Bakst, who had advised him not to come to Paris, agreed after a visit to La Ruche that his pupil's colors "sang." They did sing, as he painted in rich primary colors his memories of Vitebsk and his childhood there in such works as *The Soldier Drinks*, *The Flying Carriage*, and *I and the Village*. The latter is one of the artist's best-known works. It is a rich and marvelous evocation of his hometown, a foreshadowing of many of the themes — the peasants, flowers, cows, churches, and farmers — that would haunt him throughout his lifetime. At first, the painting seems complicated. It is made up of interweaving circles and triangles. Nothing is realistic: a small peasant girl is standing on her head; the large face of the man who dominates the right side of the painting is green; a scene of a maid milking a cow is superimposed on the head of a cow. There is a row of houses — two of them upside down — and a church with a priest's face.

The more we examine the painting, the more we discover in it. It isn't logical,

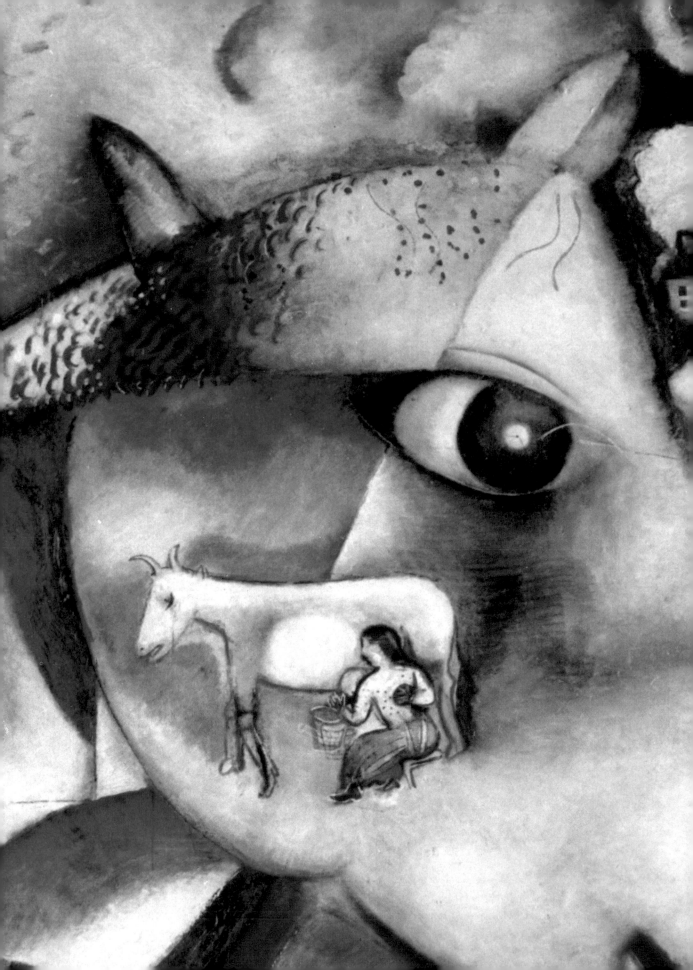

but painting is not logic any more than poetry is. If a poet can distort words, use them for sound rather than literal meaning, or disregard the usual rules of punctuation and even spelling, so can a painter have the freedom to employ forms and colors and perspective in the manner he feels best suited to the effect he wants to achieve. "Every poet has the right to say that a swallow soaring up to the sky is a dagger," the French painter, Georges Braque, wrote. "Should we painters not also have the right to paint a dagger instead of a swallow?"

Given the poetic quality of his paintings, it is not surprising that Chagall's genius was first recognized by poets rather than by painters. Nor is it surprising that during the four years he spent in Paris among his most important friends were two of the most daring and innovative poets of the time, Blaise Cendrars and Guillaume Apollinaire.

The Swiss-born Cendrars was perhaps Chagall's closest friend during those years. Two months younger than the painter, he had spent a few years in St. Petersburg and spoke Russian fluently—this alone helped create a bond between the two men since Chagall's French, though acceptable, was not yet fluent. But it was their art that really united them. Cendrars, a man of enormous energy, had just returned from a trip around the world when he met Chagall at La Ruche. He was immediately enchanted by his paintings. He felt close to them, just as Chagall found echoes of his own thoughts and feelings in Cendrars' poetry. The two spent hours together—"His shining eyes alone could console me," Chagall wrote—and the poet provided Chagall with the titles of several of his paintings, among them *I and the Village* and the haunting *To Russia, Asses and Others.*

Chagall's relationship with Apollinaire was less intimate, but of even greater importance to his career, since the poet was not only one of the leading literary figures of the period, but also one of France's most influential art critics. Apollinaire, a stocky man with a sharply pointed nose and gentle mysterious eyes, was brilliant and witty. The two men soon became friends. In spite of this friendship, Chagall was at first afraid to show Apollinaire his paintings.

The Soldier Drinks. 1911–12

Chagall has said that if we think the soldier is drunk—because his cap is flying off and because of the title—we are wrong. He is drinking tea, and the real mood of the painting is signaled by the tiny soldier with a girl on his knee at the bottom.

Apollinaire was a spokesman for and defender of Cubism, the controversial artistic movement which had its origins in France around 1907. Artists, led by Georges Braque and Pablo Picasso, began to reduce objects, figures, and even landscapes to their basic geometric forms and present them as such on canvas, at first giving little or no importance to color. Of course Chagall, to whom color and fantasy were of the greatest importance, was no Cubist.

Nonetheless, he need not have feared Apollinaire's reaction to his work. The sensitive poet was moved by the young Russian's paintings, his sense of humor, and his unique poetic vision of the world. He wrote of him: "He is an artist of enormous variety . . . not encumbered by allegiance to any theory." And he dedicated a poem to him, in which he described Chagall as having hair "like the trolley cable across Europe arrayed in little, many colored fires." He became Chagall's loyal supporter.

Though the poets appreciated him, the public failed to respond to Chagall's art during these four years in Paris. Since he was a follower of no particular school of painting (though he came under many influences, including Cubism, in such works as *I and the Village, Homage to Apollinaire,* and *Half-Past Three*) and his paintings could not fit into any of the currently fashionable classifications, his paintings did not sell. Although they were exhibited not only in Paris, but also in other cities of Europe, they were hardly noticed. Things were so bad that when one friendly dealer spoke of buying one of Chagall's paintings being shown as part of an important public exhibition *if* no one else bought it, the artist could only reply, "Why wait?"

At last, in 1914, Chagall gained some of the recognition he sought. It came not in France, however, but in Germany. In March 1913, his loyal supporter Apollinaire had introduced him to Herwarth Walden, a German poet, critic, and art dealer who, he believed, would understand and appreciate Chagall's art. A small, owlish man, with long flowing hair, Walden had both a passion for and excellent taste in art and literature. In Berlin, he had founded an influential

The Flying Carriage. 1913

Although Chagall described this as a peaceful scene, it shows a village store on fire. (The sign over the door means "shop" in Russian.) A man rushes with a bucket to put out the flames while another man is pulled into the sky by his horse, probably frightened by the commotion.

Overleaf: **Pregnant Woman**. 1913

See how Chagall has pictured an entire family here? The woman has two faces, her own and that of a bearded man on the side; her left hand points to her unborn child. (Even the goat in the sky seems to be pregnant.)

avant-garde magazine called *Der Sturm* (*The Storm*), as well as an art gallery by that name, in which he had exhibited the works of, among others, Chagall's friend Robert Delaunay. Walden traveled frequently throughout Europe, where he discovered (and later published the graphic work of) some of the most exciting artists of the time.

It was during one such trip that Apollinaire urged Walden to visit Chagall's studio at La Ruche. The dealer was deeply impressed and immediately agreed to exhibit three of the painter's works in a group show scheduled for September 1913, and to show more of Chagall's work in the gallery the following April. And, most important of all, Walden offered Chagall his first major one-man show, to be held later in June 1914.

This was the opportunity Chagall had so eagerly awaited. He enthusiastically made plans to go to Berlin for the opening and to continue on to Russia for a brief visit—to attend the wedding of one of his sisters and to see his beloved Bella, with whom he had corresponded regularly—before returning to France.

Chagall arrived in the German capital in May 1914 to prepare for his exhibition, which was to open in early June. It was to be a huge one: forty oil paintings as well as 160 works on paper, including watercolors and drawings. The gallery was so crowded with work that even the tables and part of the floor were covered with drawings.

The response of the critics and the public were all that the young artist could have wanted. Singled out for special praise was a canvas he had painted in 1913, *Paris Through the Window,* his tribute to the city in which he had been born a second time.

Instead of remaining in Berlin to enjoy his first success, however, Chagall boarded the train for Russia on June 15, the day after the opening. Before he left, he sent a postcard to Robert Delaunay in Paris which read:

"It is warm, it is raining, sauerkraut. German girls are quite extraordinarily not pretty. I am leaving today: Vitebsk. . . ."

— 4 —

Back Home Again

Marc Chagall returned to Russia a changed man. Of course, he had matured in four years, but he had been transformed by more than the mere passage of time; it was his contact with Paris and the real discovery of his art that had done it. Because of Paris and its people and the artists and poets he had met there, he would never again be the same.

Before he had left Vitebsk, he had thought of the town as a kind of prison from which he had to escape. Now he found it "strange" and "boring" and "unhappy." He felt lost, surrounded by aunts and uncles who kept telling him how big he had grown, and he eagerly looked forward to returning to the gaiety and excitement of Paris. But, because of events beyond his control, his planned short visit home became a very long one. In August 1914, Germany declared war on Russia, and World War I soon engulfed all of Europe. Travel was impossible, and Chagall was trapped.

Unable to remain inactive, he turned to his work, determined to make the best of his enforced stay in Russia. His task, as he saw it, was to record every aspect of life in Vitebsk. He succeeded brilliantly; in one year he completed almost sixty paintings and drawings.

He painted furiously—everything and everyone in sight—so that his portrait of Vitebsk might be a complete one. He had no studio of his own, but wherever he went—from one rented room to another—he took his paints and brushes and worked. One of his most memorable paintings of the time, done from the window of a room he had rented from a policeman, is called *Over Vitebsk*. It shows the snow-covered street below, and, to the right, the impressive Iltych church. What makes the work especially characteristic of Chagall is the presence of an oversized figure—in this case, a bearded old man with a sack on his back—hovering in the sky over the street. Other works of this period include portraits of members of his family, as well as a number of striking self-portraits. In addition, he completed portraits of rabbis and old Jews at prayer, as well as studies of children, beggars, and landscapes of Vitebsk and its surroundings, its narrow streets and its interesting buildings.

If Chagall's art flourished against all odds, so did his romance with Bella Rosenfeld, which had managed to survive the four years of separation. While apart, they had faithfully written to one another, and when Marc returned to Vitebsk, Bella had just finished her studies in Moscow. Their reunion was a joyous one: they were still deeply in love.

While the painter worked tirelessly on what he called his "documents" of Vitebsk, Bella brought food to his studio—at all hours of the day and night. Sometimes she brought pastries, and other times boiled fish and milk. More than that, she brought him love and inspiration, and through her Chagall learned to paint "portraits" of love—starry-eyed floating lovers, or upside-down lovers, or lovers lifted off the ground with joy. These paintings show a rare tenderness and beauty. Because of his feelings for Bella, love—the union of two human beings—became the subject for some of his most magical works.

Marc and Bella made plans to marry. The painter was certain, on the basis of his success in Berlin, that he could provide for a wife and family. Bella, determined, had succeeded in getting permission from her reluctant parents, and the date was set: July 25, 1915. Throughout the ceremony, which took place at the Rosenfelds' home, the groom was ill at ease. But his Bella was beside him, and he gained strength from her then, as he would throughout their almost thirty years together.

The newlyweds spent the first month of their life together in a small village not far from Vitebsk. It was, Chagall wrote, not a honeymoon but a "milkmoon," for

Over Vitebsk. 1914

Chagall's memories of life in the village where he was born remained strong with him throughout his long life. But, as we know, when he painted it he often let his imagination roam. Who is the bearded man floating over the town? According to one scholar, the Yiddish expression for a beggar who goes from door to door is "He who walks over the city." Another, quite different explanation may be found in Chagall's autobiography, in which he describes the Biblical prophet Elijah as arriving on earth disguised as a "stooped beggar with a sack on his back and a cane in his hand." In the end we have to use our own imaginations to discover what the artist wished us to understand.

his wife kept serving him good country milk. But this idyllic period soon came to an end. In August, the artist asked the governor of the town for permission to return to Paris with his bride, but the necessary exit visa was refused: the war was still being fought. Instead, Chagall was faced with the prospect of serving his country. He would either have to join the army as a soldier or find work that could excuse him from military duty. Initially, he applied to the army for assignment to a camouflage unit, where his skills as a painter might be utilized, but he was rejected. As an alternative, Bella's brother, an important lawyer in charge of the department of war economy in St. Petersburg, was able to offer him an office job, related to the war effort, that would exempt him from the life of an ordinary soldier.

Marc and Bella moved to St. Petersburg and found a small room to rent. Though Chagall was bored with his job—he was an inept bookkeeper and hopeless at doing any paperwork—this assignment nonetheless allowed him to stay out of soldier's uniform and come home each night to his beloved Bella.

The job also allowed him, because it required little of his time, to paint throughout the war years and to meet and show his work to some of the richest and most influential collectors in Russia, many of whom bought his paintings. The number of serious art collectors, especially in the Jewish community, was growing, and Chagall did his best to interest them in his work. Through them and through exhibitions in Moscow and in St. Petersburg, his reputation spread as one of the most prominent artists in Russia, a respected leader of the new ways of painting.

As his fame grew and articles about his work were published, so did the scope and nature of his art. He spent much of his free time in the countryside, and scenes of country life became a theme of his paintings. In 1916, a daughter, Ida, was born, and the beautiful child became the subject of some of the artist's most gentle portraits. The horrors of war, too, were reflected in his work; tired, anguished soldiers provided the subject matter for many of his paintings.

At the end of 1917, the Russian government signed an armistice agreement with Germany, leading to Russia's withdrawal from the war. At any other time, such an agreement would have caused Chagall to seize the chance to return to France, but an event of even greater significance to him—the Russian Revolution—drove all such thoughts from his mind. Earlier in the year, the Russian people had risen up against the Czar and forced him to abdicate. On November 7, the Bolshevik workers, led by Lenin, completed the Revolution; they seized power and established a "dictatorship" of the proletariat (the common people), a communist state.

As a consequence of this revolution, the rights of full citizenship were restored to all of Russia's Jews. They would no longer be persecuted and forced to live under the harsh conditions that had been imposed upon them during the reign of the Czars. Jews would be free to live and travel wherever they wanted; they could work at whatever jobs they chose. "Something was about to be born," Chagall wrote in his memoirs. This was no time for him to leave the country of his birth. Instead, as a respected, successful artist, and as a Jew, he wanted to take advantage of this freedom and hoped to play a leading role in the artistic life of the new Russia.

Double Portrait with Wine Glass. 1917

In another celebration of his love for Bella, Chagall pictures his bride holding him aloft while he raises a toast to their happiness. Above, an angel offers its blessing.

Right: **Bella with Flowers**.

It was a period of enormous excitement. Artists and writers and actors gathered together, enthusiastically making bold plans for the future. All kinds of proposals were made to give intellectuals a greater role in the country's future. There was talk of a new Ministry of Culture and even mention of Chagall heading it. Bella, however, was strongly opposed to such an appointment. She felt that it would distract him from his work. At her urging, the painter took his wife and daughter back to Vitebsk, away from the chaos and tumult of post-revolutionary Petrograd. If he was to play an official role in the cultural revolution that was sweeping through Russia, he would do so from Vitebsk, where life was more peaceful.

An opportunity to play just such a role presented itself within a few months. Shortly after his return to Vitebsk, Chagall had worked out a plan to create a new art school there and had sent it to Anatole Lunacharsky, the Commissar of Education and Culture in Moscow. Lunacharsky was impressed, and on the basis of the plan he appointed the painter as Commissar of Art for Vitebsk. Chagall's task—to turn his town into a flourishing art center—was a challenging one. Though his primary responsibility was to establish and become director of the new school of fine arts, he was also empowered to organize museums, exhibitions, lectures on art, and all other artistic ventures within the city and region of Vitebsk. He attacked his job with his usual enthusiasm and energy. Nothing was too difficult for him. Even before officially taking office, he organized a large exhibition of paintings by Vitebsk artists. Included were works of his former teacher, Yehuda Pen, and his friend Victor Mekler, as well as five of his own paintings, among them the joyful *Double Portrait with Wine Glass,* which shows Chagall seated on Bella's shoulders, with an angel floating above the couple.

It was an impressive exhibition, but Chagall's first chance to show just what the artists of Vitebsk could do came in November 1918, on the first anniversary of the Revolution. It was to be a day of celebration, marked by parades and festivities throughout the Soviet Union. To demonstrate its vitality, Chagall brought together all of Vitebsk's artisans and craftsmen. The center of the town was joyously decorated: shops and trolleys were newly painted in red, purple, yellow, and green; colorful flags, banners, and posters lined the streets, and Chagall's own designs (some of them executed by men who usually painted houses) were everywhere in evidence. The people of Vitebsk were invigorated and excited as they had never been before, and the man who had organized this triumphant ceremony took special pride in the smiling faces of the workers as they marched through the town. Chagall had achieved his purpose: to bring art into the streets of Vitebsk.

Official reaction, however, was less enthusiastic, and Chagall was angrily criticized by leaders of the newly formed Communist party. Why was the horse

Years after the exciting days of the Russian Revolution of 1917, Chagall drew his recollection of celebrations in the streets.

green? Why was the cow flying through the air? What did all this have to do with the Revolution or with Lenin? Some critics even solemnly noted how many sets of underwear could have been made with the material they felt had been wasted on the flags and banners.

Though disappointed by this official reaction, Chagall was not surprised. He had known from the very beginning that he could no more rigidly follow any political doctrine than he could completely follow any artistic doctrine. He was an artist, a free man, and whatever the party leaders said, he was determined to work toward his goal of establishing Vitebsk as an important center of the arts.

In spite of strong opposition from those who believed that government funds were better spent on less "cultural" endeavors, Chagall managed to raise the money necessary to realize his dream. By 1919, both a new museum and an academy of the arts were ready to open. Chagall was most interested in the school. The museum represented the past and the present; the Free Academy was concerned with the future, and it was there that he would turn the young people of Vitebsk into the creative forces for the years to come.

Under his energetic leadership, and with the help of teachers he recruited from all over Russia, the Academy expanded rapidly. Before long, there were six hundred students. Chagall himself was loved and respected by these young people, and an amusing slogan was heard throughout the school: "God grant that everyone may *chagalle* like Marc Chagall." (The Russian word *chagalle* means "march forward.")

Nonetheless, not everyone was enthusiastic about Chagall's efforts. Outside the Academy, he was attacked by conservatives who felt that students should be taught to paint works that realistically depicted the life of the country and its

Bella sat for another loving portrait by her husband in 1934. Chagall called the painting *Bella in Green*.

people and not the creatures of imagination that peopled Chagall's work. Inside the Academy, there was an even more serious threat from Kasimir Malevich, one of Russia's best known painters. Malevich, who developed the art movement known as Suprematism, had been asked by Chagall to teach at the Academy in late 1919. Malevich's art and ideas were completely different from those of Chagall. He and his followers were experimenting with an art that was pure and geometrically abstract. They disapproved of Chagall's "story-telling" through his art and his use of vivid colors. Gradually, the school became divided into two camps, and the rivalry between the two artists became increasingly bitter. It reached a climax when, following a trip to Moscow, where he was soliciting funds for the Academy, Chagall returned to Vitebsk to find that the sign above the door of the school had been changed from Free Academy to Suprematist Academy. Enraged by this betrayal on the part of colleagues he himself had brought to the school, he sent in his resignation at once. Many students and faculty members begged him to remain, but his mind was made up. Unappreciated at home, he was determined to leave both the Academy and Vitebsk. He was bitter, and later expressed his anger in his autobiography. "I won't be surprised if . . . my town obliterates all traces of me and forgets the man who, laying aside his own paint brushes, worried, suffered, and took the trouble to implant Art there. . . ." he wrote. He never again returned to the city of his birth.

In May 1920, Chagall settled in Moscow. Though he was known as an artist and as a cultural leader throughout Russia, he had earned little money. Because of this, he and Bella and Ida were forced to live in one small, damp room. There were terrible food shortages, and it was sometimes impossible to get milk for the child. But Chagall had known poverty before and felt certain that he could overcome it once again. Somehow, he would find a way to make a living.

The move to Moscow did have one positive side: it offered Chagall the opportunity to fulfill a dream to work in the theater. Years before, in St. Petersburg, he had been asked to submit ideas for a theatrical production, but these had been rejected as too radical. Now, in Moscow, he met Alexis Granovsky, a man who had the vision to go along with these ideas.

Granovsky had recently embarked on a new venture. In an attempt to bring vitality and freshness to Jewish culture, he had founded a State Jewish Theater, which, when Chagall met him, had just moved to new quarters in Moscow. For the occasion, the painter was asked not only to design the sets and costumes for the company's new production, but also to execute a mural for the theater's auditorium. Given a free hand by Granovsky, Chagall took over every aspect of the production. He created the sets, the costumes, the makeup, and even choreographed the movements of the actors. It was an exhausting job, but an exhilarating one; and its enormous success justified all the work the artist had put into it. Equally successful, too, was Chagall's auditorium mural, *Introduction to the Jewish Theater*, a joyful representation of clowns, acrobats, musicians, and actors, which even included an image of Chagall himself.

In spite of this artistic triumph, Chagall continued to earn little money. Granovsky was unable to pay him for his work in the theater, and buyers for his paintings were hard to find. Unable to support himself and his family, he was forced to accept a position in a war orphans' colony near Moscow. Teaching these sad young people how to paint was a satisfying and often moving experience, but it could not become his life's work. He was a painter, and he had to paint, but there seemed to be no place for him in Russia.

Soon, however, he learned that there was a place for him outside Russia. In 1922, a letter arrived from a friend in Berlin: "Are you alive? There is a rumor that you have been killed in the war. Do you know that you are famous here? Your pictures are selling for very high prices. . . ."

The letter was decisive. Discouraged by his attempts to gain recognition in Russia, he would return to Western Europe to further his career as an artist. He loved his homeland, but he was again forced to leave it. The Russians, he felt, didn't need him. "They don't understand me. I am a stranger to them," he wrote.

5

On to the Future

In the summer of 1922, Chagall left Russia. His first stop was Berlin, where he confirmed what his friend had written: he was famous in the German capital. Throughout the war and after it, Herwarth Walden had continued to exhibit his work, and many of his paintings had been sold to private collectors. There had been a number of articles about him, and his fame had spread, as had his influence on many young artists. But there were disappointments, too. For one, Walden was either unwilling or unable to tell him where his paintings were, both the sold and the unsold. For another, the money that he had earned through the sale of his paintings was far less than he had expected.

Nonetheless, Chagall remained in Berlin for a year. Well known and respected, he was able to make friends among the important critics and artists working in the German capital. Of these, the most important to his career was Paul Cassirer, a distinguished art dealer and publisher. Cassirer had learned that, while in Moscow, Chagall had completed an autobiography he had worked on over the years. He read the text and proposed to publish it—together with twenty etchings he asked the artist to create to accompany the autobiography. Chagall accepted the commission with enthusiasm. Etching—drawing with a steel instrument on a wax-coated copper plate which is then etched with an acid in preparation for printing—was a new technique for him. He mastered it in a remarkably short time. Even though Cassirer never published the text of the autobiography, he did publish a portfolio of Chagall's etchings in 1923, a poignant record of his childhood and early years in his native land.

Much as he profited from his stay in Berlin, Chagall remained eager to reach

Green Violinist. 1923–24

his final destination—Paris. While in the German capital, he had learned that he was as famous in Paris as he was in Berlin. Furthermore, during the summer of 1922, he was informed that the greatest of all French modern art dealers, Ambroise Vollard (who was also a publisher), had seen his paintings and was anxious to discuss a major new project with him. On September 1, 1923, Chagall, this time with Bella and their seven-year-old daughter Ida, was back in his artistic birthplace, Paris. He felt he had come home.

The painter's return to Paris in 1923 marked the beginning of a period of artistic and personal success that came to an end only in 1941, with the outbreak of World War II. Shortly after his arrival, he paid a call on Vollard. The meeting was a success; in the course of it, the legendary dealer who had encouraged so many promising artists asked Chagall to illustrate Nikolai Gogol's *Dead Souls,* one of the greatest Russian novels of the nineteenth century. He also agreed to pay the artist whatever he needed to complete this new set of etchings. Chagall was overjoyed. He loved Gogol's book, and Vollard's generous offer freed him from all financial worries.

Vollard's decision proved to be an inspired one. Because of his own background, Chagall was uniquely qualified to bring to life through his art Gogol's satire of Russian peasant life. In the 107 illustrations that he etched between 1923 and 1927, he lovingly conveyed the warmth and poetry of his homeland and depicted its often larger-than-life people. It was the first of several successful collaborations between Vollard and Chagall. Though the results of these collaborations were only published after Vollard's death—he was more interested in having the artist create the work than he was in making it available to the public—these distinguished achievements in a new technique would place Chagall among the most accomplished graphic artists of modern times.

While working on *Dead Souls,* Chagall also found time to paint. He found inspiration not only in his memories—*Green Violinist,* for example—but increasingly in the varied French countryside which had inspired so many great

The Rooster. 1929

Chagall's love for animals is nowhere more obvious than
in this graceful painting of a woman clad in red tights (a
performer?) tenderly embracing a smiling rooster. Echoing
the theme of love is a couple in a rowboat.

Peasant Life. 1925

Wherever he was, Chagall's memories of life in his native
village provided subjects for his art. This dreamlike
painting was made in a small French village that must
have reminded the artist of home.

painters. Whenever they could, he and his family traveled—from the rugged French Alps to the rolling, colorful hills of the south—discovering and growing to love their new homeland. Never before these travels had he painted nature so poetically. Rural scenes, barnyard animals, blue seas, and, above all, color-splashed flowers became prominent in many of his paintings—among them the lyrical *Ida at the Window,* a masterpiece that shows the artist's delight with the trees and flowers of the French countryside.

This newly developed knowledge and understanding of nature—of plants and animals—was undoubtedly among the factors that led to Vollard's next idea: that Chagall illustrate the seventeenth-century French classic, the *Fables* of Jean de La Fontaine. Chagall and La Fontaine, one of the most beloved of all French writers, seemed a perfect combination to the artist and to Vollard, but much of the French public was horrified. These affectionate, charming tales, in which talking animals—crows, ants, mice, and others—take on human characteristics, were taught in all French schools as examples of the clarity and beauty of the French language and spirit. How, these critics argued, could a Russian Jew capture this uniquely French quality in his illustrations? Vollard paid no attention to these objections. The indignant critics had ignored the fact that the fables had not been invented by La Fontaine, that most of them had been adapted from early folk tales (such as those of Aesop), or more modern ones, many of which originated in the East. They were not French but universal.

Chagall's etchings for the *Fables,* one hundred of them executed between 1927 and 1930, were another masterful achievement, but even before he finished them he and Vollard agreed on the next work to be illustrated: the Bible.

The artist approached this awesome task with reverence and enthusiasm. The Bible and its characters had been an unforgettable part of his childhood in Vitebsk. Yet, to do his job well he felt it necessary to go to the land of the Bible—to Palestine—to feel at first hand the spirit and poetry of the Bible. He arrived in Palestine (which was to become the state of Israel in 1948) in February 1931, and remained there for nearly three months. It was an unforgettable experience. Totally captivated by the Holy Land, he felt the past and present come together as one. He rediscovered the faces of his childhood, and they, and the dazzling light that shines upon the Holy Land, found their way into his paintings, among them *Synagogue at Safed* and later works such as the powerful and moving *Solitude*.

When the artist returned to Paris, he began work on the Biblical etchings. He was to work on them for many years (they were not completed until 1956). These 105 illustrations, a twentieth-century artist's reverent interpretation of the Old Testament, are considered by some to be among the great inspirational works of art of all time.

During the 1930s, the Chagalls did a great deal of traveling outside France. In 1932, a visit to Holland enabled the artist to study the paintings and etchings of the Dutch master, Rembrandt. On a trip to Spain, he was deeply moved by the works of the Spanish masters, Diego Velàzquez and Francisco Goya, and in 1937, on a visit to Italy, Chagall had an opportunity to study the works of the great Italian artists—Bellini, Titian, and Donatello, among others—in the museums of Florence. Contact with these great masterpieces of the past strengthened the painter's art and added a seriousness to it.

Because Chagall, like many creative artists, drew inspiration from the work of his predecessors, these trips were of great significance to him. However, a trip to Poland in 1935, where he had been invited to attend the inauguration of a Jewish cultural center in Vilna, had special meaning for him. There, only two hundred miles from Vitebsk, he once again came in contact with the life of the Jews of Eastern Europe. What he saw and felt saddened him profoundly: these Jews and their way of life were again threatened, this time by a wave of anti-Semitism that was sweeping Europe. An element of apprehension and tragedy entered his work. Burning villages and fleeing peasants became the subjects of his paintings, and blacks and grays often replaced the bright colors for which he was known.

His fears for the future proved to be well founded. German troops invaded

Poland on September 1, 1939, beginning World War II. Two days later, England and France declared war on Germany. An all-out effort had to be made to stop the aggression of Hitler's Germany, which threatened to overrun Europe.

Chagall had lived through war and revolution, and he knew the destruction they wrought. He had already felt the effects of the turmoil. In August 1939, he and his family had gathered up his work and moved to a small village not far from Paris, where he felt there was less chance of danger. But danger was to follow wherever he went. By the spring of 1940, the situation had worsened. Denmark, Norway, Belgium, the Netherlands, and Luxembourg were invaded by the German armies. It was clear that the battlefield would move to France, and that the area near Chagall's home would most probably be a major line of defense

Overleaf: **Solitude**. 1933

The title of this painting describes it perfectly. The religious Jew, holding the Torah in his arms, seems to sense a tragedy to come, just as the artist himself might well have in 1933, when the existence of Jews all over Europe began to be threatened by the Nazis in Germany.

Here, Chagall illustrates one of the most moving Old Testament subjects—the angel stopping Abraham from obeying the command to sacrifice his beloved son Isaac.

Time Is a River Without Banks. 1930–39

Chagall worked on this painting when Europe was in
turmoil. Many images of the artist's past are here, even a
pair of lovers, but they all seem more disturbing than
joyous, expressing his fears for the future.

for the French forces. It was time to move once again, this time to the south of France, where they found a home in the ancient village of Gordes, near Avignon, in the region of Provence.

On June 22, little more than a month after they bought their home, France surrendered to the German army. It was a dark period for the whole free world, and it was a dangerous one for all Jews, who had become the prime targets of Hitler's madness. In spite of the risk to his life and that of his family, Chagall, hoping that France would drive out the enemy, remained in Gordes for almost a year. He dreaded the thought of once again leaving the country in which he felt so much at home, stubbornly refusing all efforts to convince him to emigrate.

Of these efforts, the most serious and tempting came in the form of an invitation from New York's Museum of Modern Art, brought to him by Varian Fry, the American director of the Emergency Relief Committee, an organization whose purpose was to bring the most important European intellectuals to safety in America. The museum also invited other painters whose lives were endangered, such as Pablo Picasso, Georges Rouault, Raoul Dufy, and Max Ernst.

Chagall was bewildered by Fry's argument that his life was actually threatened as long as he remained in France. Furthermore, the idea of crossing the ocean to go to America was frightening. It was too far away and he knew nothing about it. "Are there trees and cows in America, too?" he asked Fry.

In spite of Fry's assurances that there were, Chagall at first refused the generous offer. In April 1941, however, when France adopted severe anti-Semitic laws and the Nazi-dominated French government began rounding up Jews and sending them to prison, the artist changed his mind. It was a difficult and painful decision, but he realized he had no choice.

On May 7, 1941, Bella, Ida, and Marc Chagall, weary and frightened, left France, crossing the border into Spain. From there they traveled to Lisbon, Portugal, where they waited until they found space on a cargo ship that would take them to America. The crossing lasted forty-three days.

—— 6 ——

The New World

The Chagalls arrived in New York on June 23 in search of a new home, one in which they might live until the war came to an end. The Germans had invaded their first home, Russia, only the day before. They were refugees, among the many thousands who had been driven from their countries by the threat of Nazi persecution and had found asylum in the United States.

Chagall was among the more fortunate of these uprooted, displaced people, many of whom were penniless and without friends or family. His painting was well known in America from reproductions in art magazines and from several important museum and private collections; he had a dealer and friend, Pierre Matisse, son of the great French painter Henri Matisse, who was willing to show his work in his New York gallery and help spread his fame. He was warmly greeted, too, by other members of the American art world as well as by many old friends who had also taken refuge in the United States. Furthermore—and this was a great consolation—he had managed, through complicated efforts by his daughter Ida, to send ahead all of his paintings, drawings, and studies, packed in trunks and weighing 3,500 pounds, which enabled him to set to work at once, completing paintings he had been working on for years.

In spite of these advantages, Chagall found life in New York difficult. He was overwhelmed by the immensity of the great city, its towering skyscrapers, and its dizzying pace. In the seven years during which he lived in and around the city, he never came to feel at home there. He knew no English, and because he refused to learn it—preferring to speak French, Yiddish, or Russian—he lived mainly in a world of displaced Europeans. Prominent among these were the large number of

Russians, who had settled temporarily in New York, and whose company made Chagall feel closer to Russia than he had for many years.

It was through one of these, the great Russian choreographer Leonid Massine, that Chagall received his first important job in America. He was asked by the Ballet Theatre of New York to design the scenery and costumes for a new ballet conceived and choreographed by Massine. The story of the ballet, *Aleko,* was based on a nineteenth-century poem, *The Gypsies,* by Alexsander Pushkin, the greatest of all Russian poets. The music was by Tchaikovsky, the greatest of all Russian composers. It was the ideal assignment for two Russians working in America; it enabled them to recreate their homeland from memory among the skyscrapers of New York.

Because of an invitation by the Mexican government, the first performance of the ballet was to be given not in New York but in Mexico City in September 1942. To prepare for it, the Chagalls and Massine arrived in Mexico during August. As he had done in the past, the painter involved himself in every aspect of the production. No detail, no minor prop escaped his attention. Bella again was of great help, supervising the making of the costumes, based on Chagall's sketches, while the artist himself painted the four huge backdrops he had conceived.

At the ballet's opening, the Mexican audience was enchanted by the production. Music, poetry, movement, and color had been combined into a glowing whole. Time and again, Chagall was called back to acknowledge the cheers. It was in every way a triumph, a triumph that was repeated at its New York première one month later.

Once back in New York, Chagall resumed his painting. Many of his canvases showed the influence of the strong, vivid Mexican colors and light. Though his work in the theater prevented him from traveling extensively while there, he had managed a few short excursions. Other works were more somber and troubled, reflecting his concern for the suffering of the land of his birth.

The Dream. 1939

A woman lying on a bed in a room without walls, is comforted
by a bearded, Christlike figure. An angel, hovering above,
reaches out to her. Could this be a dream of death?

Angel and the Reader. 1930s

Even though their official home during these years in America was New York, the Chagalls spent a great deal of time in the country, outside the city. For the summer of 1944, they rented a home at Cranberry Lake, in the Adirondack Mountains. There, on August 25, they learned that Paris had been liberated from German rule. They were elated; the war was not yet won, they knew, but they felt certain that the end was near and that they would soon be able to return to their home in France. In the midst of their elation, however, personal tragedy struck. Only a week later, Bella took ill, and what seemed to the doctors in the Cranberry Lake hospital a minor virus infection was in fact a deadly infection that took her life on September 2, 1944.

It was a shattering loss for Chagall. For nearly thirty years Bella had been his companion and his inspiration, as well as his most perceptive critic. Following her death, he wrote: "A loud clap of thunder and a burst of rain broke out at six o'clock in the evening on the 2nd of September, 1944, when Bella left this world. Everything went dark before my eyes."

Chagall was unable to work for nine months. He spent his time in his studio, his canvases turned to the wall. When, after these months of solitude and grief, he began to paint again, his work was often melancholy and subdued, reflecting the enormous loss he had suffered.

A chance to recover from his depression and loneliness presented itself in 1945 when the Ballet Theatre of New York again commissioned him to design the scenery and costumes for a ballet. This time it was *The Firebird,* based on an old Russian folktale and danced to the music of another Russian, the contemporary composer Igor Stravinsky. There was an enormous amount of work involved, as there had been for *Aleko.* Chagall, as always, gave himself completely to the job. This time, his daughter Ida, now twenty-eight years old, was at his side, supervising the making of more than eighty costumes as Bella had once done. The production, which opened in New York in October 1945, was another great success, evidence of the artist's determination to seek a new life.

That life, as Chagall had always hoped, would be lived in France. On May 7, 1945, Germany surrendered, ending the war in Europe. A few months later, when Japan surrendered, World War II came to an end. Chagall's dream of returning to Paris was becoming a reality. In the spring of 1946, following a large exhibition of his work at New York's Museum of Modern Art and the Art Institute of Chicago, Chagall returned to Paris for a visit. The following year, he returned to the French capital again, this time for an exhibition of his work at the Musée National d'Art Moderne. In 1948, he returned to France for good, grateful for all America had done for him but happy to be home.

By this time, his position as one of the important painters of his time was secure. Important exhibitions of his works were held throughout Europe — in London, Amsterdam, Zurich, Berne, and Venice. As always, he continued to work hard, wherever he went. In 1949, he moved to the south of France, to the delightful town of Saint-Jean-Cap-Ferrat. The following year he bought a home, Les Collines (The Hills), in Vence, a small town above the Riviera, where he worked among the fruit, flowers, and scents of the Mediterranean countryside.

On July 12, 1952, a few days after his sixty-fifth birthday, Chagall married Valentine (called Vava) Brodsky, a Russian-born woman of great charm and intelligence, with whom he shared the rest of his life. They had met only six months before, through the painter's daughter.

His life had been an extraordinarily rich one, but rather than merely contemplate his past achievements, he looked toward the future and new artistic challenges. For the remainder of his very long life, he continued to paint with

Le Champ de Mars. 1954–55

The title of this painting refers to the location in Paris of the Eiffel Tower, seen at the upper right. Chagall's memories of his childhood and his more recent past come together in a vivid work.

War. 1964–66

Chagall was almost eighty years old when he completed this
large and powerful painting depicting the horrors and tragedy
of war.

vigor, expressing on canvas his love for the world of nature and animals, for music and for dance, and for the circus. His themes remained the same — floating, embracing lovers, flying cows and horses, sparkling bouquets of flowers — but his canvases were larger, and his colors more dazzling than ever. He returned to Biblical subjects as well and painted a series of huge canvases.

But Chagall, a man of enormous energy, was not content to spend the rest of his life merely painting on canvas. He worked in the theater again, designing sets and costumes for a ballet in Paris in 1958, and for an opera, Mozart's *The Magic Flute,* for New York's Metropolitan Opera in 1967. He also created a huge circular painting that decorates the ceiling of the great Paris Opera House and two enormous murals for the Metropolitan Opera House at Lincoln Center.

Late in life, his creative curiosity drove him to seek new means of expression for his art. "I work in whatever medium likes me," he said. He began to execute sculptures in clay and in stone; he created ceramics, mosaics, and tapestries. Even more remarkable, at the age of seventy he began to master the intricate and difficult art of stained glass, which was especially suited to his brilliant and translucent colors. His windows, which he worked on over a period of twenty years, enrich buildings and churches in France, Switzerland, Germany, England, the United States, and Israel.

On July 7, 1967, Chagall celebrated his eightieth birthday. He had no time for formal celebration. At an age when most men feel their work has been completed, the artist was looking toward the future.

The next decade was marked by more creative challenges — he never slowed down — and by further honors. In 1969, Chagall helped organize a huge retrospective exhibition of his work at the Grand Palais in Paris, which included paintings, drawings, ceramics, sculpture, tapestries, and stained-glass windows — representing every period of his creative life.

Four years later, in 1973, a new national museum was inaugurated in the south of France. Set on a hillside overlooking the city of Nice, it houses one of the artist's most impressive achievements, the Biblical subjects—paintings, drawings and sculptures—he had worked on over a period of thirty years, grouped together under the title "The Biblical Message of Marc Chagall."

That same year, Chagall was able to fulfill one of his dreams by returning, for the first time in over half a century, to the land of his birth. Honored throughout most of the world, the artist had been practically ignored in the Soviet Union. The occasion for his return was an official invitation by the Minister of Culture, who had organized an exhibition of Chagall's early work at an important museum in Moscow. It was a moving and often tearful experience for the painter, an opportunity to see again his early work and to rediscover his roots. When, after the eleven-day visit (which took him to Moscow and Leningrad, but not to Vitebsk), he returned to France, he felt elated and rejuvenated by this encounter with his past, which had always remained a part of his work.

Chagall's ninetieth birthday was celebrated throughout the world in 1977. For the artist it was an important and busy year: he was awarded one of France's most valued honors, the Grand Cross of the Legion of Honor; he visited Italy and Israel; and he worked on stained-glass windows for the Art Institute of Chicago. Most significant, however, was another exhibition of his work at the Louvre, France's most respected museum, showing sixty-two paintings executed during the previous decade, while he was in his eighties. They were acclaimed by critics as some of the artist's finest work, a brilliant testimony to his creative vitality.

In the years that followed, important exhibitions were held in Europe and in America, and a major retrospective, tracing each step of his long career, opened in London in January 1985, giving testimony to his vast achievement. On March 28, three days before the exhibition closed, Marc Chagall died at his home in the south of France. He was ninety-seven years old. A poet-painter, he created for us a colorful world of floating lovers, of flying cows, and of fiddlers on the roofs. In depicting this world of fantasy and delight, he made certain that his place in the history of art would be very real and secure.

List of Illustrations

SERIES EDITOR: Robert Morton

EDITOR: Edith M. Pavese

DESIGNERS: Dana Sloan and Laura Lovett

PHOTO RESEARCH: Lauren Boucher

——— LIBRARY OF CONGRESS CATALOGING-IN-PUBLICATION DATA ———

Greenfeld, Howard.
Marc Chagall / by Howard Greenfeld.
92 p. 19 × 25.7cm. — (An Abrams first impressions book)
Summary: Examines the life and work of the painter whose Russian Jewish background did
not prevent him from making an international search for his own ways of expression.
ISBN 0-8109-3152-4
1. Chagall, Marc, 1887-1985—Juvenile literature. 2. Artists-Russian S.F.S.R—Biography—
Juvenile literature. [1. Chagall, Marc, 1887-1985. 2. Artists. 3. Painting, Russian. 4. Art
appreciation.] I. Title. II. Series.
N6999.C46G7 1990
[92]—dc19   89-6447
                                                                           CIP

——— PHOTOGRAPH CREDITS ———

The Art Institute of Chicago © 1990 10, 82; Myles Aronowitz 45; David Heald 2–3, 32,
43, 67.